I'm on the Way to a Brighter Day

We always have to remember that
it's up to us —
we're the ones
that have to push
the clouds away

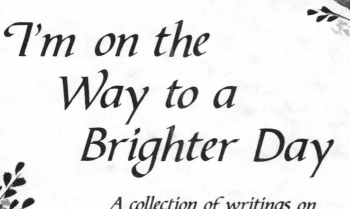

I'm on the Way to a Brighter Day

A collection of writings on
feeling good about yourself and
making your life the best it can be

by Douglas Richards

Blue Mountain Press ™

Boulder, Colorado

Library of Congress Number: 83-073535
ISBN: 0-88396-202-0

This book was written by Douglas Richard Pagels.
Thanks to the Blue Mountain Arts creative staff,
including Jody Kauflin and Faith Hamilton, and
thanks to Diane Westlake.

Manufactured in the United States of America
First Printing: January, 1984

Blue Mountain Press INC.

P.O. Box 4549, Boulder, Colorado 80306

Dedication:

To parents who strive to
give their children both
roots and wings, as mine
have lovingly given me.

Introduction

Life doesn't always play by the rules. Sometimes despite your best intentions, disappointment can come around more than it should and fulfillment can seem like a far-away goal. If you've ever experienced these feelings, you're not alone. Everyone has their gray days, and no one is spared from the realization that life isn't easy.

From time to time, we all get troubled with personal problems, doubts and anxieties. But don't ever think that you've got to accept more than your share of problems, and don't ever think that you've got to go through them alone. There's always someone to turn to. Your friends. Your family. Your love. And, of course . . . yourself.

So many wonderful possibilities reside within you. The ability to change, to grow, to give, to love. The opportunity to be happier than you've ever been. To live in a world that is warmed by your desires and your dreams. It's true! The possibilities are really within reach . . . if only we could take the time to travel in their direction. As one of my favorite philosophers (Woody Guthrie) once said, "Most everybody I see knows the truth; but they just don't know that they know it."

I'm on the Way to a Brighter Day is written as a reminder of a sane truth in a crazy world: that there is something positive, fulfilling and necessary to be accomplished. And it begins with a glimpse at ourselves and a vision of what we want to be. When all is said and done, we have ourselves to live with. Our hang-ups. Our inner selves. Our outward appearances. Our doubts and beliefs, our fears and our failures, our hopes and our dreams.

Anyone who aspires to being happier and more rewarded than they imagined possible discovers that the source of their satisfaction comes from within. The hope, the desire and the movement all originate within and shine outward from there. As we progress, our heads and our hearts show us more truths about ourselves and our potential every time we take the time to see.

When you're on the way to a brighter day, wonderful things begin to happen. Your inner perspective increases, and you start to see things in a different light. Your attitude changes. You begin to see the good and believe the best. You reach a point where you're not so vulnerable; you're not shattered by disappointment, you live with it and grow from it. You find the beautiful results of liking yourself and relating that self to others. You build up your confidence and your capability, and by so doing, build a better life as you go and as you grow.

As with all journeys, the difficult part is to begin. It is a sincere and special wish that this book will take you a step along the way . . . to a brighter day that is waiting just for you.

Don't Ever . . .

Don't ever try to understand everything —
some things will just never make sense.
Don't ever be reluctant to show your feelings —
when you're happy, give into it!
When you're not, live with it.

Don't ever be afraid to . . .

. . . try to make things better —
   you might be surprised at the results.
Don't ever take the weight of the world
   on your shoulders.
Don't ever feel threatened by the future —
   take life one day at a time.

Don't ever feel guilty about the past —
    what's done is done. Learn from any mistakes
    you might have made.
Don't ever feel that you are alone —
    there is always somebody there for you
    to reach out to . . .

Don't ever forget that you can achieve
    so many of the things you can imagine —
    imagine that! It's not as hard as it seems.
Don't ever stop loving,
    don't ever stop believing,
        don't ever stop dreaming your dreams.

The opportunity to grow
and achieve our dreams
is always there.
The possibilities to be happier,
wiser, wealthier, healthier,
more involved, more alive,
more confident, more responsive,
more of the person *you* want to be . . .
  are possibilities that are
    around each bend in the road.
It's up to us to *begin* the journey.
That's the hard part.

Don't think
of how weak you are.
Think of how strong
you're going to be.

Try to choose the road
that is right for you.
Once you've made the choice,
trust your intuition.

As you begin, believe in your
choice and your direction, and
tell yourself that . . .

I'm on the Way

I'm on the way to
    finding out some answers that I need.
I'm on the way to better things . . .
        like reaching out for hopes and dreams,
            like getting to know myself,
                and finally getting ahead in life.
I'm on the way to becoming
        more of the person I am inside;
            a person that wants
                to learn and grow and experience.
I'm sure it won't be easy . . .
I know there will be challenges to meet
        and decisions to make,
            but I know now, too,
        that even the difficult and trying times
            can actually be to my benefit.
Wherever I may go, I'll take with me
        confidence and love and courage,
because I'm on the way
            to a brighter day . . .
                and I know I'm going to find it!

Beginning Today

I will begin this day anew, with the thought of becoming the person I'd like to be; if not completing that difficult journey today, at least getting a little further along the way.

Today I will set aside some time just for me . . . to plan, to dream, to be honest with myself about myself; to become better acquainted with this person that I am, and this place that I call home.

Today I will experience something new. I will learn from the world around me, from the words I read, the sounds I hear, the touches I feel, the faces I see. Even through the course of my daily tasks, I will try to lean toward understanding, try to make the commonplace a wondrous place to be.

Today I will think of my friends and be warmed by the thought; of my loved ones and try to show them all the love that I feel.

Today I'll thank the people and places that have helped me along on my way, the friendships and smiles, the hardships and trials, that have made me what I am today.

Today I'll remember how naturally happiness comes to the person who thinks it should be.

I'll remember how — by some interesting twist — doing for others is also doing for me. I'll remember that having a sense of humor has helped me to survive. I'll remember when everything else seems to go wrong, that I'm glad of life, of living this day . . . I'm happy to be alive.

Today I will listen to my inner needs and comply as best I can: with a little learning for my mind; as much love as my heart can hold; nourishment and exercise for my body; seeing all the beauty of the world for my soul.

Today I will think of the past only long enough to learn from it; the future only for a fleeting dream.
Today is my day;
this minute is mine . . .
I'll make it work for me.

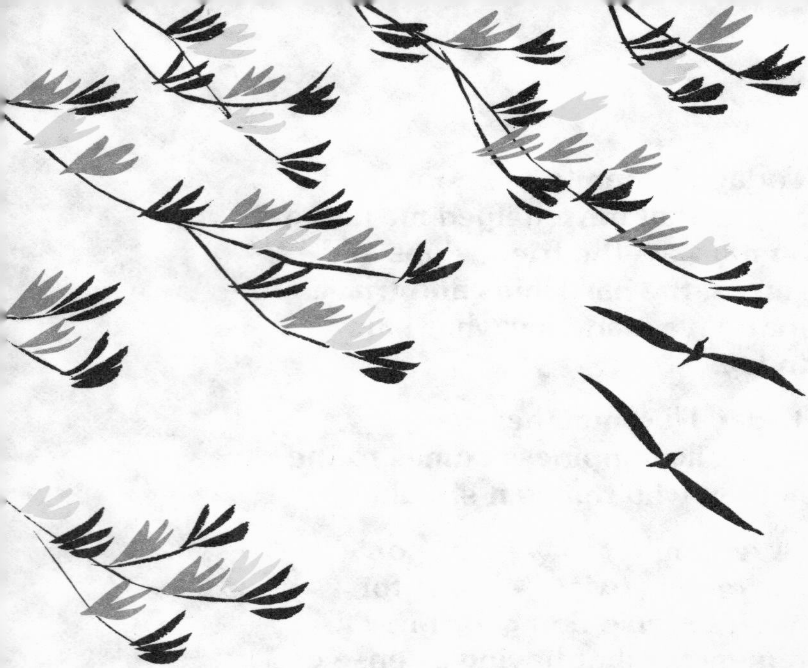

There is a miracle in the making.
And the miracle is you.
You . . . awakening the beauty within;
seeing things in a new light;
taking the time to
    make your body healthy;
making your mark so the right things
    will happen;
setting the stage for the pleasures
        and promises of love;
developing the special talents
    you have been given;
expressing your own creativity
    in the way you are living.

Know . . . this day . . . that there has
always been a wonderful you,
and life will help you grow
    if you let it.

Believe . . . tomorrow . . . that you will
create an even healthier, happier you,
    and the best will only get better.

Will I ever be
as happy again
as I was when I was a child?
Maybe it would help
if every now and then
I let the child that shines within me
live in harmony
with the adult
I'm required to be.

An invitation to happiness

It's nice to be creative.
It is essential to do what you can
to create your own personal environment —
    one that works for you.
Create it with your own thoughts
    and your own actions.
Receive your desired results
    and don't settle for less.
Accomplish what you want to achieve.
If it is writing a book, write the book.
If it is sewing a quilt, sew the quilt.
Piece all the chapters of your dreams together;
combine all the efforts of your creativity,
and thread them all together
into a wonderful reality —
    designed especially for you . . .
                                by you.

Adventures are there for the taking . . .
but I have to be the one
   with the willingness to explore.
The possibilities for happiness
   are endless . . .
but I have to be the one to believe
   in their possibilities and make them mine.
Love is there for the making . . .
but I have to be the one to trust
   in its magic and believe . . . before
   I can ask my love to trust forever in me.

I have to be the one to make the difference.
I can see things as I wish them to be.
And since I want a successful life warmed
with happiness and love,
I will do whatever is within my ability.

Never until now have I wanted to make
   such a positive change in my days.
Never again will I take things for granted —
   my life is waiting for me
      to get involved in the making
         of its wonderful ways.

There is so much
that can be encouraged
    and accomplished
in the years of our lives
    in the days of desire
        in the hours to be . . .
Let us shape our days
into the best times
we can possibly imagine
    with our courage
        and our hopes
            and our dreams.
We can rise above it all.
We can find a place
    where our problems
aren't nearly as tall,
    where our hope isn't
        nearly so small

and where things go our way
    because we're going
        with the flow
            of the way things should be.

A View of the World

There are always
two ways of looking at things.
Some people see only the clouds;
the smart ones know
    about the silver lining.
I'd like to think that life
gives us every opportunity
to put things
in the proper perspective . . .
    to see the horizon of tomorrow
    beyond our own limited view,
    and glimpsing at the things
        that are truly important.
The general rule seems to be this:
    that unhappiness is usually
        the result of shortsightedness;
while the real joy of living
    is to be found in so many
        places of our world . . .
    It all depends
        on how you look at it.

Don't look for your
gratification
to come in a lump sum.
Look for it in the little ways,
and save each one
for you.

Don't miss the miracle.
Don't be so involved
in trying to *be* a success
that you forget that you . . .
in your own unique and wonderful way . . .
already *are* a success.

I don't know much
      about philosophy,
   but I do know this:
         that we get out of life
         what we put into it,
and we can always do more and be more . . .
         be stronger,
            more enduring,
            more happy . . .
         than we *think* we can.
Let's *think* less
         and *imagine* more.
Let's realize that each day
brings with it
         the miracle of a new beginning.

Color Your World

So few things seem to be black and
    white anymore.
So few clear-cut cases of "Yes, I should
definitely do this," or "No, I can't do that."
These days, this world, this moment in time
presents us with so many possibilities
and choices.
Choosing isn't always easy, but it *is* nice
to know that the choice is ours.

For me, I choose to color my world.
I want it to be green and growing
    and full of natural ways to live.
I want it to be gold and glowing and peaceful,
    flowing toward completeness. . .

I want it to be colored in the warm light of love
    and the soft shades of friendship.
I want my world to be alive with
    the colors of passion and compassion,
        celebration and strength,
and the beautiful results of trying to make
    my own little world
        a better place to be.

I don't want to
    go "over the rainbow" . . .
I want to bring
    a little bit of the rainbow
        to me.

This I Believe

I believe that life is for living . . .
  for rising in the morning with
    a smile on my face
from the simple joy of being me
     and being alive.
I believe that my success in this day
  will depend on my outlook,
    my openness and my optimism.
I believe that this day
  offers possibilities
    to change for the better,
  and opportunities
    to reach for the best.
I believe that real happiness
    is all around me, and that
      it is as near as the
      voice of my friend,
        the whisper of my love,
     and the thought of my family.
I believe that eyes
    are made for beholding,
  arms are made for unfolding,
    and hearts are meant to say . . .
That for all its wrongs and worries,
  my life is right for me,
  and thanks to my efforts,
    it will only get better . . .
  this I truly believe.

We can never become
so discouraged
that we can't see
the road in front of us.

Lost paths
are found again.
Your fears,
your insecurities,
your shortcomings
   may shadow you for awhile,
but eventually will be dissolved
      in the light of a new day
         and the direction of a new way.

One step equals one move
in one positive direction.

You never know
until you try.
And you never try
   unless you *really* try.
You give it your best shot;
you do the best you can.

And if you've done everything
   in your power, and still "fail" —
the truth of the matter is
   that you haven't failed at all.

When you reach for your dreams,
   no matter what they may be,
   you grow from the reaching;
      you learn from the trying;
         you win from the doing.

The less often we fall,
        the better.
But to never fall at all
        is disastrous.

What are we to become;
how are we to really learn
        if we never unlearn;
how are we to exhilarate at flight
        if we have only
                ever known the sky?

Remember: it's okay to fall.
        It's okay to make mistakes.

In times of trouble . . .

We all have
an inner sanctuary
we can go to . . .
and the door
is always open
and the experience
is always soothing
and the heart
is always happy
to keep you
safe and warm
until it's okay
to go out
into the world again.

You don't have to know
how to get there.
You'll find the directions
if you need them.

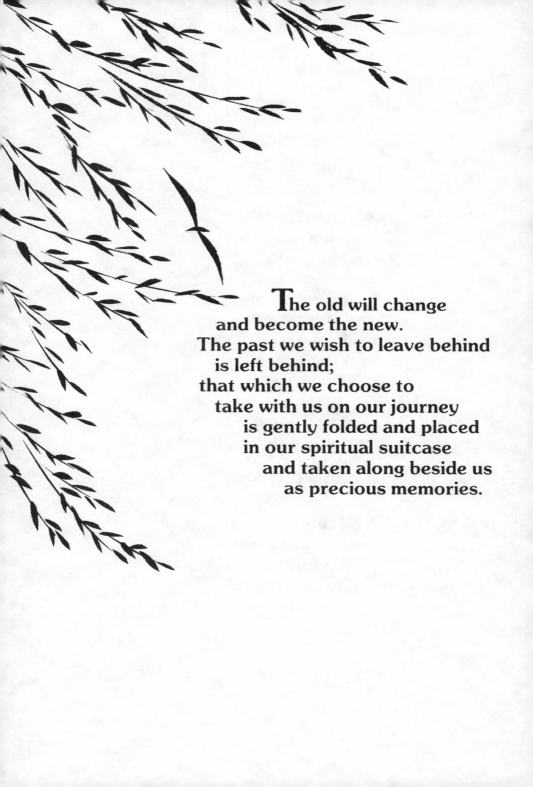

The old will change
and become the new.
The past we wish to leave behind
is left behind;
that which we choose to
take with us on our journey
is gently folded and placed
in our spiritual suitcase
and taken along beside us
as precious memories.

At times we need to stop and rest,
to gather strength, to refresh
our inner spirits. At times like these,
we wish for the others to go on without us,
telling them that we "will catch up in a
minute" while we, in a private reverie,
slip into the woods of the natural world,
absorbing a newness essential to our beings.
Soft greens. Deep blues. Air. Smells.
Breathing. At perfect peace. Beside a
quiet stream with the god almighty that
lives there.

There's a good prescription
for curing the blues. It reads like this:

Rx: Plan on staying home just one day
and enjoy yourself! If you're sick and tired
of the same old thing (and you're supposed
to be at work), call in sick. You'll be
telling the truth . . . just not the whole truth!

Get your favorite things around you —
your favorite magazines, that new book
you've been dying to read, a bit of
chocolate (for medicinal purposes only),
maybe even catch up on the latest "soaps"
on television that you haven't seen for ages.
And — oh, yes — don't forget the cat beside you.
A purring cat works wonders for the spirits.

By the end of the day, you should be feeling
all caught up, refreshed and ready to begin again.
You'll know if the prescription worked
by how much tranquility you've gained
by feeling okay about doing something
you rarely do . . .
absolutely nothing all day.

I'll bet that even
the happiest person
        in the world
feels like staying home
and hiding under the covers
sometimes.

There are times
when just being complacent
is all we can ask for.

One of the nice things
about being human
      is our tenacity.

Life goes on.
Sometimes worse for the wear,
    sometimes better for our efforts,

      but always . . .
        always . . .

          life goes on.

There's a category
for certain things
in my life
that I've come to accept.
They are the items
that are filed
under the category of
"things that just
weren't meant to be."

Sometimes it's a real juggling act . . .
trying to keep your hopes up
when the gravity of a situation
is doing its best
to get you down.

There are times when
you just have to
drop the whole thing
and start over.

The world is a wonderful place,
but it is never generous enough
to blanket us with security
and let us live life
        with stars in our eyes.
Our optimism is always
        tempered with realism.
And try as we might to keep them up,
        hopes can fade
                and stars can fall.

But every time I see a falling star,
        I'll wish for this . . .

        that you and I will never lose
        that gleam that love provides
        to hearts that continue
        to hope for the best . . .
                and very often
                        receive it.

If you can
walk away from worry
   and move toward joy;
leave behind conflict
   and move toward resolve;
part with emptiness
   and move toward fulfillment . . .
you will be taking
   a step into
      a beautiful future.

Infamous
last words:

"I'd like to,
      but I can't."

Look for the Light

When we're feeling
more lost than found,
we don't need to search around us
            for the answers . . .
    we need to remember to look within.

Within each one of us
            is a guiding light —
an instinct for survival
    a yearning for a better life
        a longing for happiness
            an ability to change
                and cope
                    and discover
                        and grow.

The possibilities are all there
lighting up our lives
        each time
            we take the time
                to believe in ourselves.

All Things Are Possible

The effort you make — however small —
   may be exactly what was needed.
The dissatisfaction you feel today
   may be the positive change
   you experience tomorrow.
The person whom you casually meet
   may become your best friend in life.
The love that you radiate —
   like lightshine to others —
   may warm you for seasons to come.

Believe in the world's wondrous schemes;
      that our desires
         our actions
            and our possibilities untold

   can take us far beyond our dreams.

Do what you can.
Every small spark of activity
has the potential to become
a flame and kindle another light
that has been
waiting to shine.
A brighter somewhere
makes a brighter everywhere.

I know that
one day,
someday,
everything that once
seemed all wrong
will be all right.

When life
throws you
for a loop
and turns your
   world around,
you just have to
turn around and face it.

If a change is required
   to deal with a new situation,
keep in mind that
you're in the driver's seat.
And if you have to change,
then you might as well
make it a change
         for the better.

We can't always choose
the direction
   life takes us in,
but we can decide
to make the most
   of the changes
      life brings our way,
and to steer a course
   towards a brighter day.

If you want to reach the
farthest peak in the distance,
you will have to go faster
    and farther than
        others along the way.

But it will be the most
    magnificent journey!

The gentle climbs along the path
will lead you to beautiful vistas that
    — even if seen a thousand times —
    would still astound you
        and hold you at peace.

My most perfect sanctuary
is found in a secret place . . . within;
   where love lives wonderfully together
      with my accomplishments
         and my defeats.
I am content with myself,
   and secure in the knowledge
      that life will be good to me.
I am aware that I am less than
   some people would prefer me to be.
I may fall short of many outreaching goals,
   but I am great in this:
I have for so many things in life
   an inner love. I have a certain something
      that makes me complete.
I have a belief in myself.
I have a belief in the wonder of people.
I have a belief in the sanctity of love.

The Most Wonderful Thing You Can Do . . .

Allow yourself to fall in love!
Being in love — the feelings, the freshness,
the exhilarating, intoxicating happiness —
is akin to opening a window on a sweet
mountain morning when the air has just
enough warmth to let you stand there —
as naked as the day you were born —
feeling like a child
in a world created especially for another child
                              and you.
It's a grand and giving experience.

Good and Getting Better

Every day is an opportunity —
an occasion to celebrate your being
   happy and healthy and hopeful.
Life is the most important thing we have.
We must not lose track of that.
It is governed by time —
and the times of our lives are meant
   to be fulfilling and rewarding.
We can help that belief to become
   a beautiful reality, or we can stand
   defiantly in its way and be unhappy.
That choice is ours to make.

Our lives will either be short or long.
We cannot choose the distance.
But we can decide how to travel along the way.
Let us walk the way with
    our friends and our family;
let us run to the arms of our love.
Let us blend together dedication and desire;
    discovering always new things about ourselves
and new ways to see the world in a positive light.

If we can do all that, then this dream
    can be fulfilled . . .
believing in ourselves and knowing every day
for the rest of our lives
    that we're better than we were . . .
        but we're getting better still.

I want to make a change

Sometimes my mind is on a thousand
different things . . . wondering how I'm going
to work things out money-wise, and worried
that I'm not doing as well as I should be.
I'm thinking that I should be trying a
little harder with some personal things,
wanting to learn more, hoping to make
things better in love and life, and
hoping that one day I'll be able to see
some real improvement.

There are so many aspects of life; so much
to think about and so much to do . . .
it gets confusing sometimes, and I get
concerned. But I refuse to let it get me down.
I don't want to feel weak; I want to feel strong.
I don't want to feel fragile; I want to know
that if I fall, I'll be able to bounce right
back again. I want to be able to grow and
adjust and discover and meet the challenges
I have to face. . . .

They say that you get out of life what you
put into it . . . and I'll be the first one to
admit that I've been standing on the sidelines
a little longer than I should have. But I
want to make a change . . .

I'm going to reach a little higher . . . and
reach again, and I may need a hand
from you every now and then.
I hope you don't mind me asking,
but I can't think of anyone else
who would give and care and
share strength the way you do.

I want to make a change . . .
and get better and
better each day through.
And if I succeed, one thing
I want to be able to be . . .
   is a better person for you.

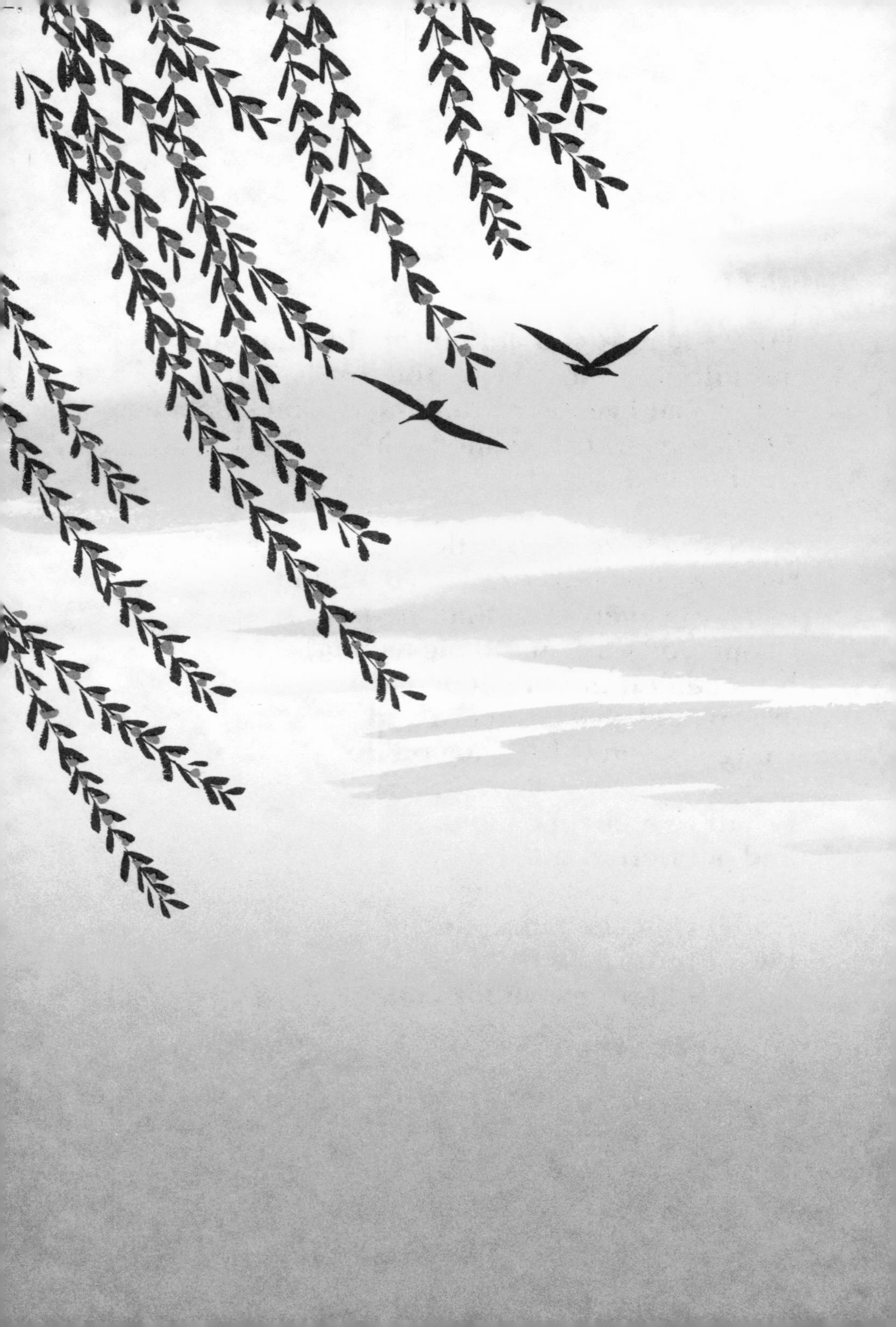

You're a winner!

There's nothing quite like belief.
Believe in yourself and you'll see!
Realize the abilities that only you possess;
 the uniqueness that was given to you;
  the special ways you are
   and the ways you can improve.
With you, there is no second best.
There are no losers in your race.
It's you . . . the winner all the way.

Whether you win by a lot
 or just a little, the decision
  is up to you.
Give yourself every opportunity.
You've got what it takes,
 and you know it.
Why not go for it?

Just see what a difference it makes
 when you believe.
 Imagine yourself succeeding . . .
  then reach for it,
   and succeed.

It's Okay

It's okay to be afraid
of the things we don't understand.
It's okay to feel anxious
when things aren't working our way.
It's okay to feel lonely . . .
even when you're with other people.
It's okay to feel unfulfilled
because you know something is missing
   (even if you're not sure what it is).
      It's okay to think and
                  worry and cry.

It's okay to do
whatever you have to do, but
just remember, too . . .
that eventually you're going to
adjust to the changes life brings your way.
And you'll realize that
it's okay to love again and laugh again,
and it's okay to get to the point where
the life you live
is full and satisfying and good to you . . .
and it will be that way
because you made it that way.